this abc book for

....

....

Trace the line ----

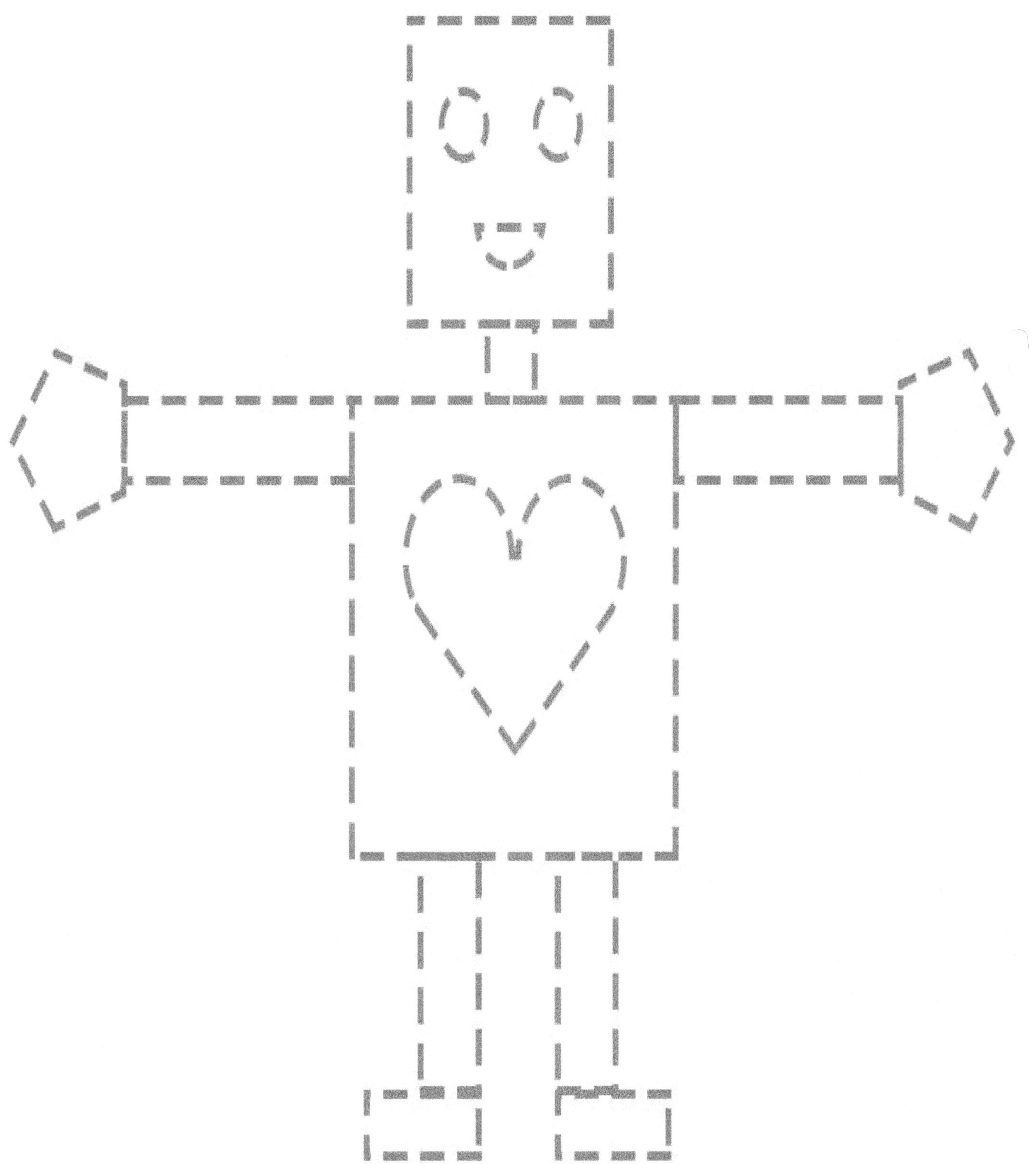

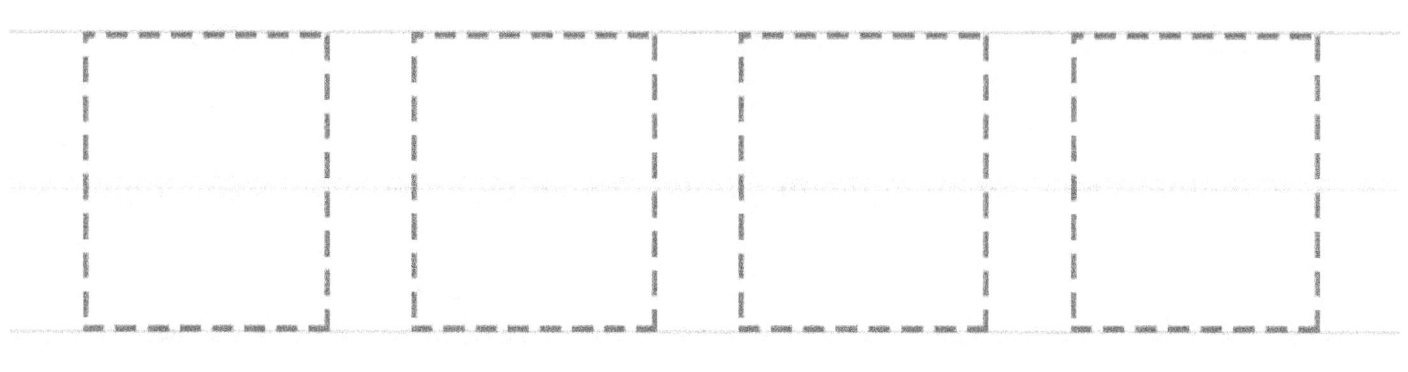
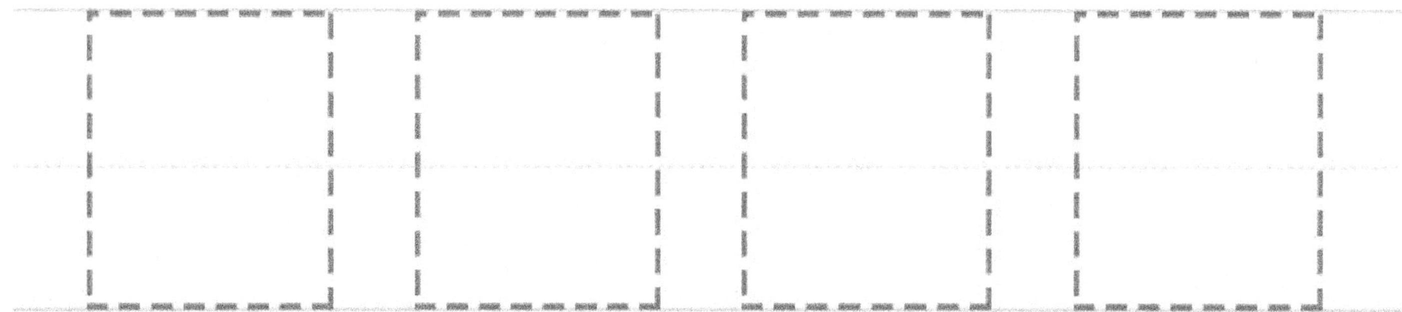

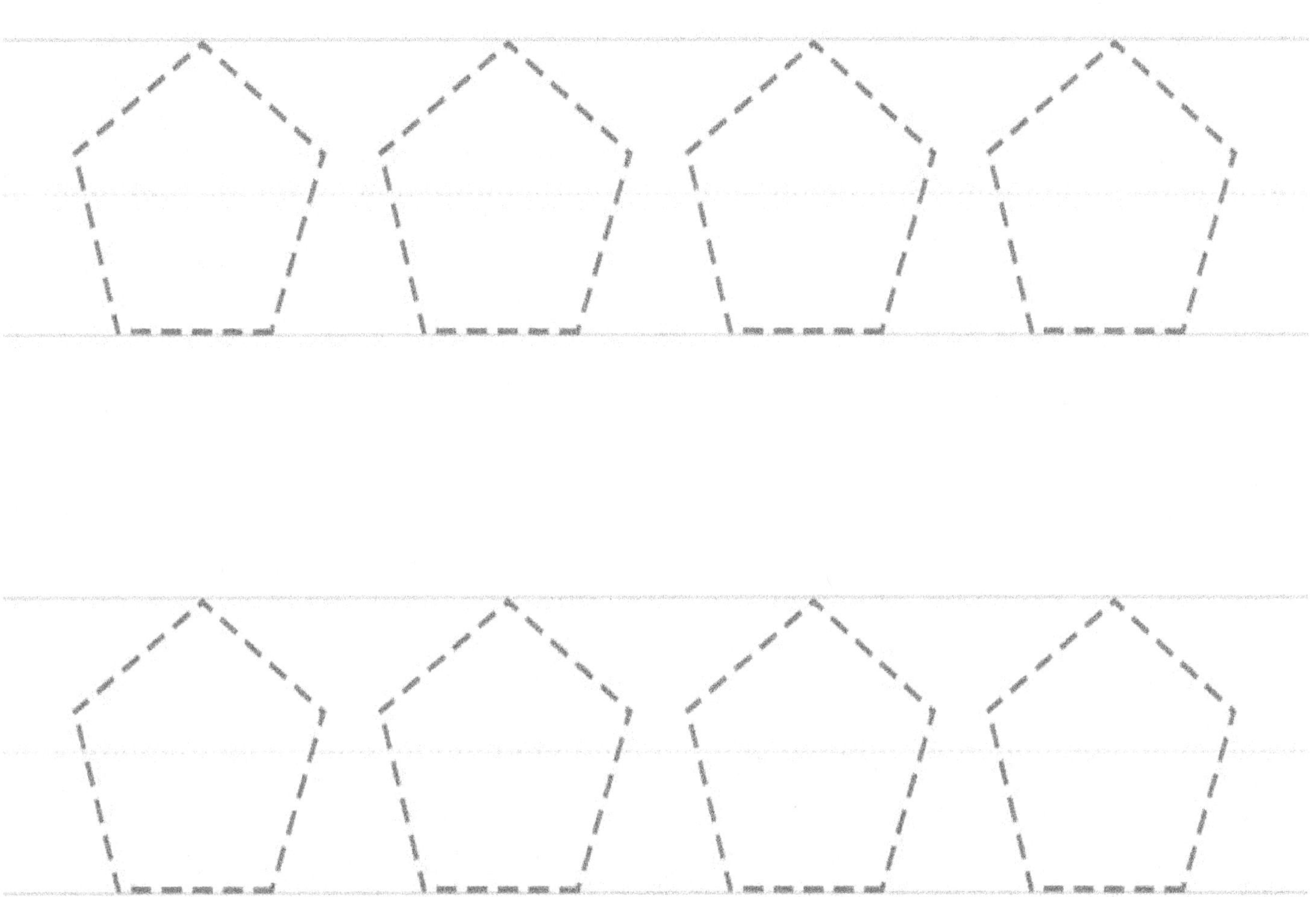

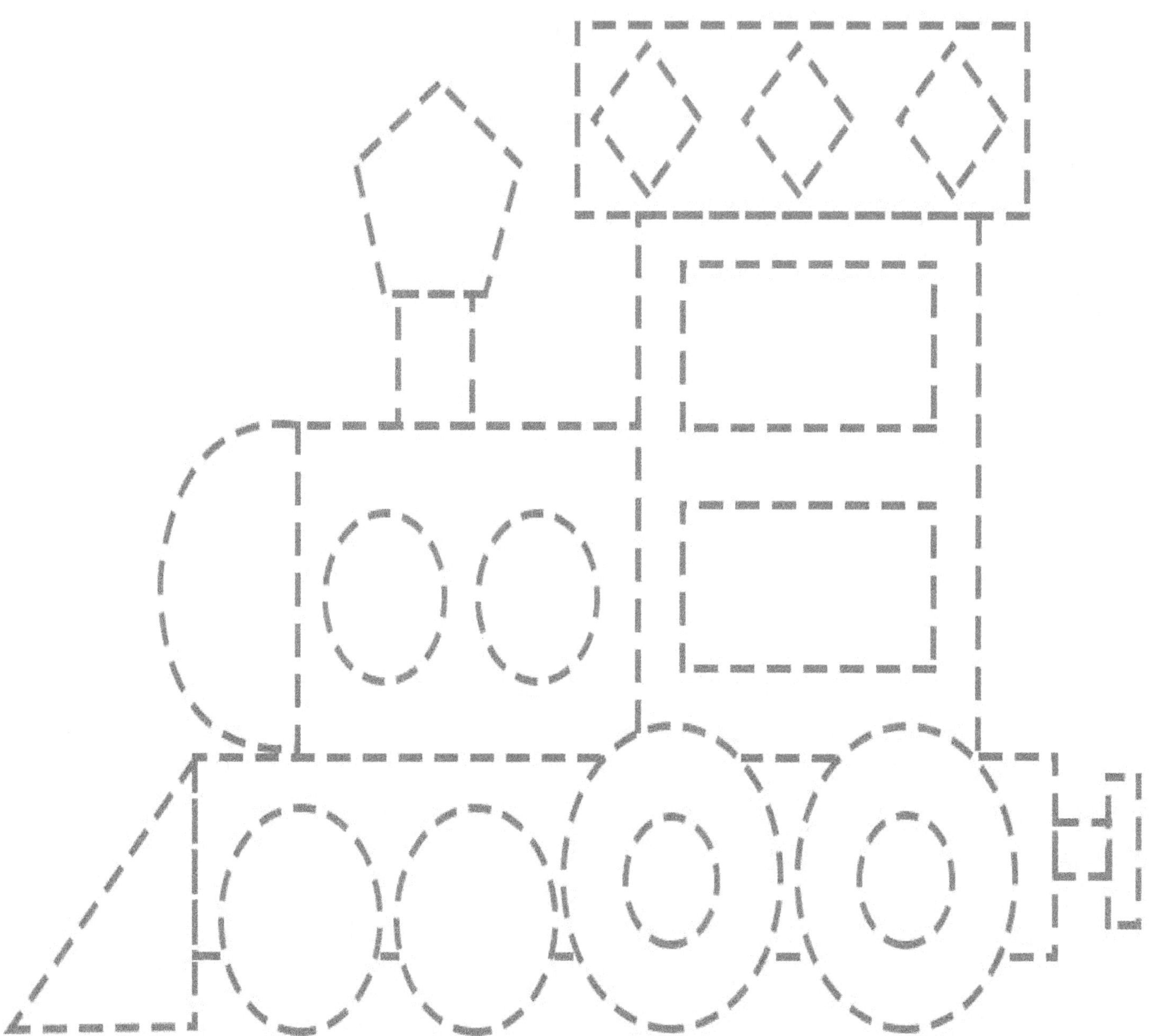

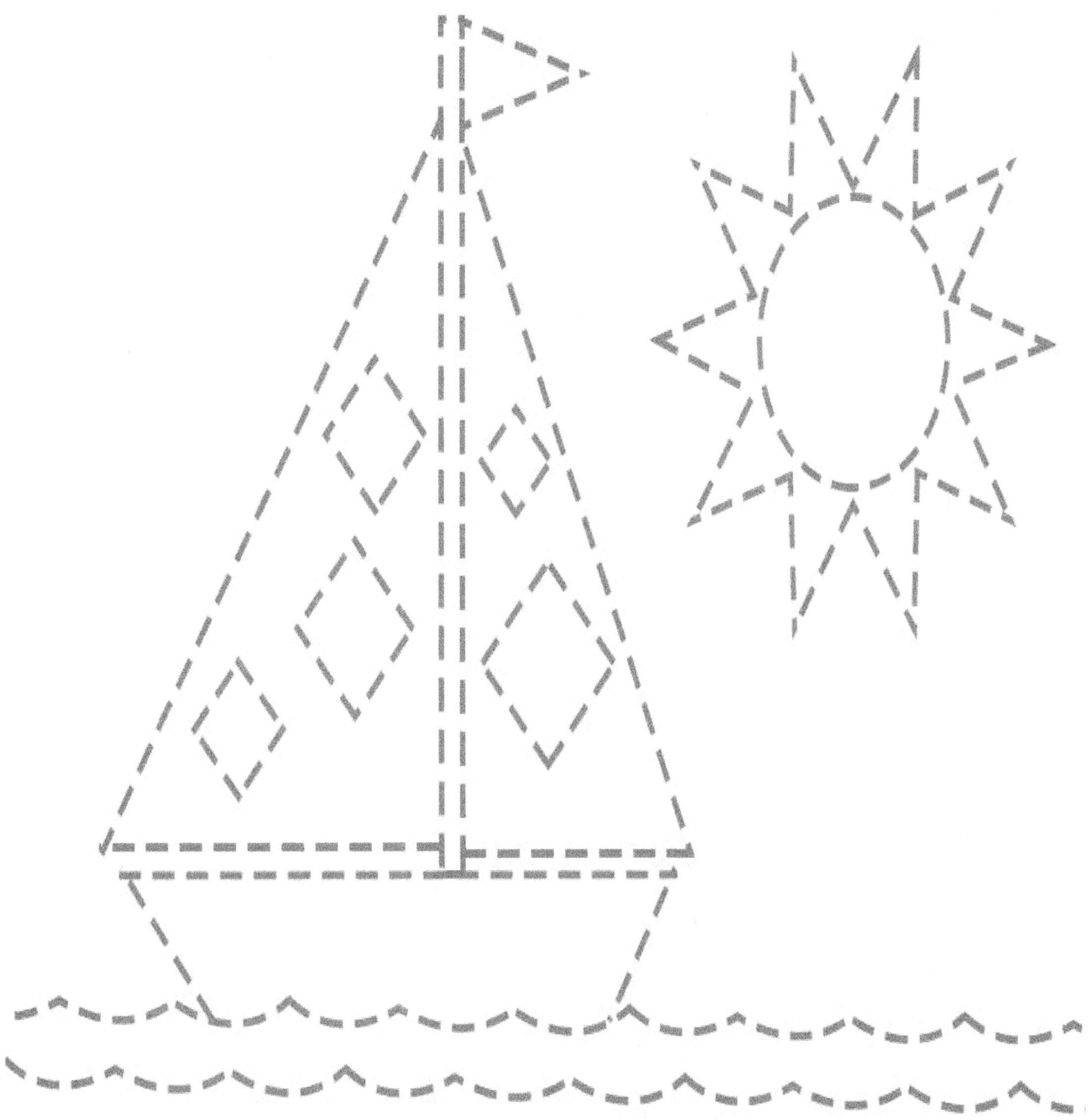

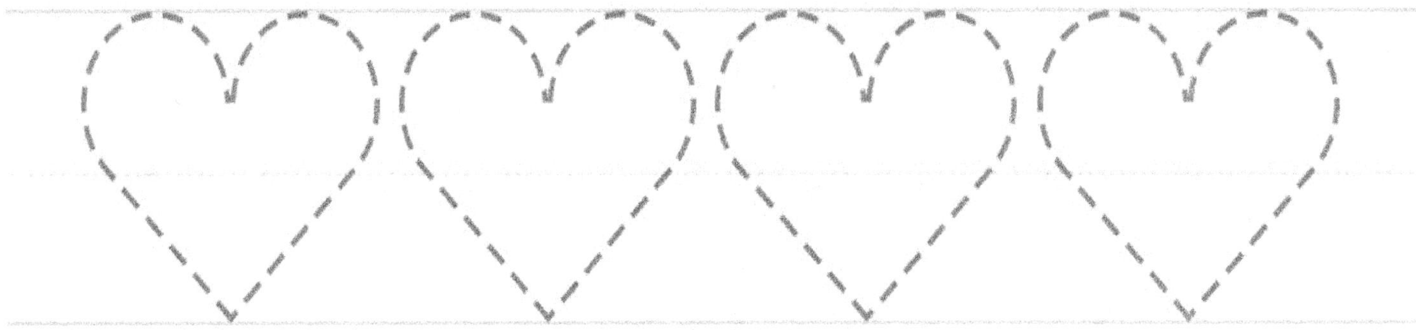

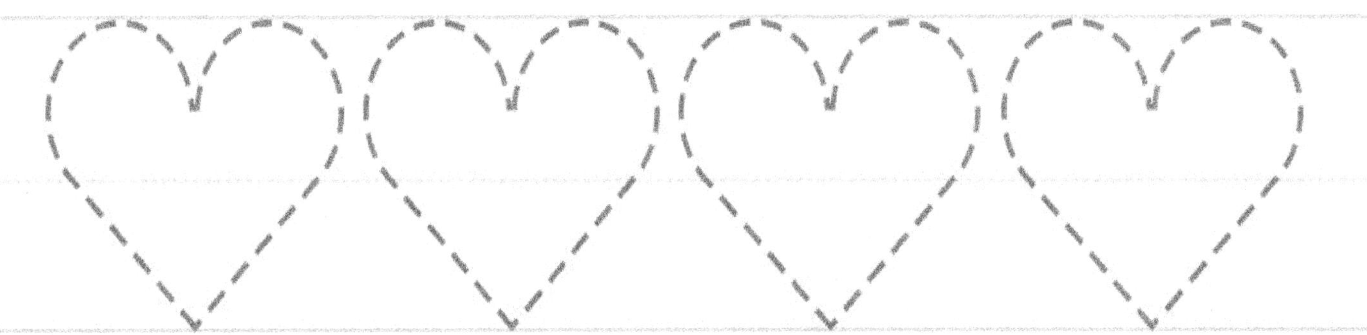

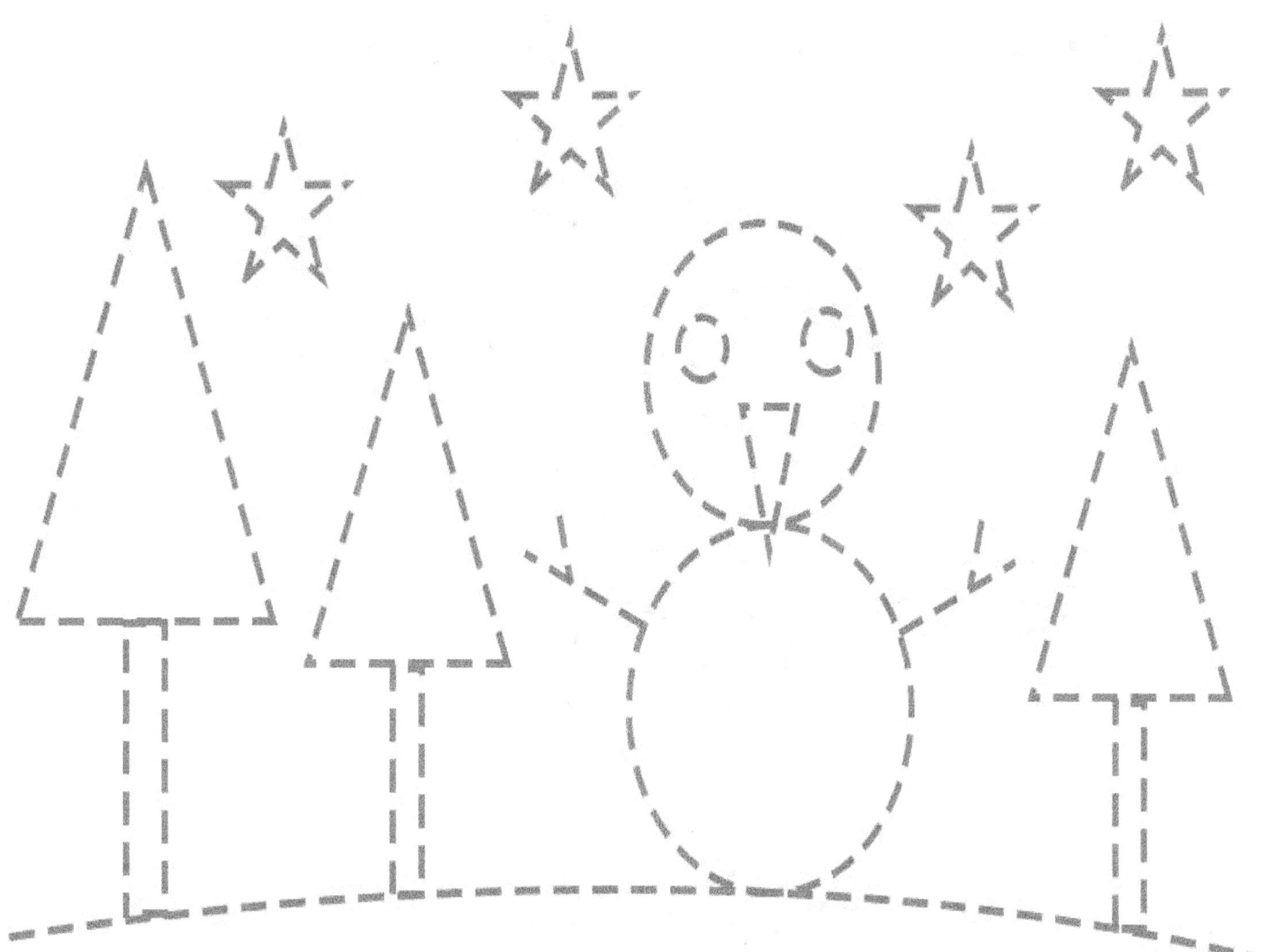

Trace and write Alphabet

A a

A a

Letter Hunt

Find and color the letter A

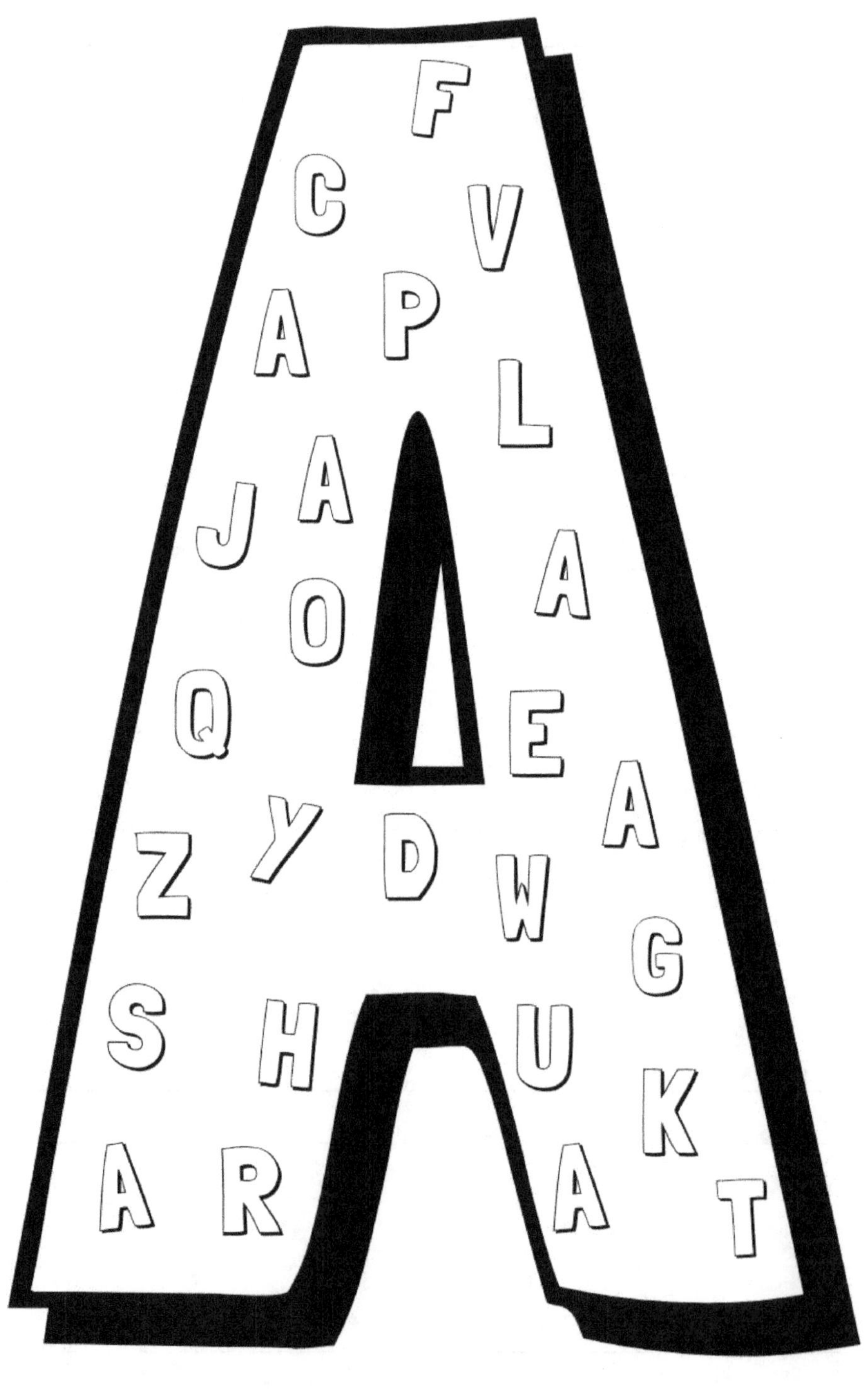

B b

B b

Letter Hunt

Find and color the letter B

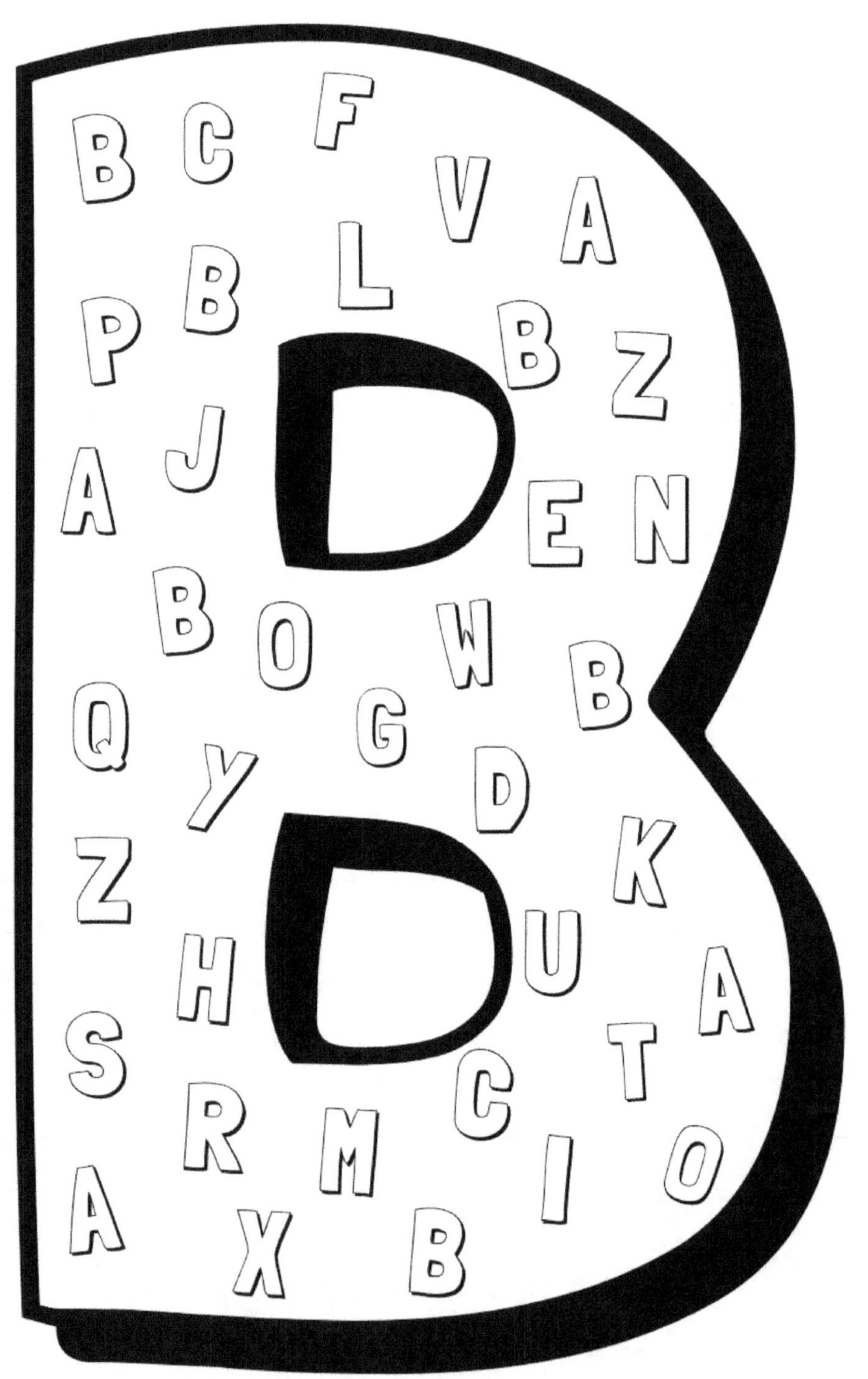

C c

C c

Letter Hunt
Find and color the letter C

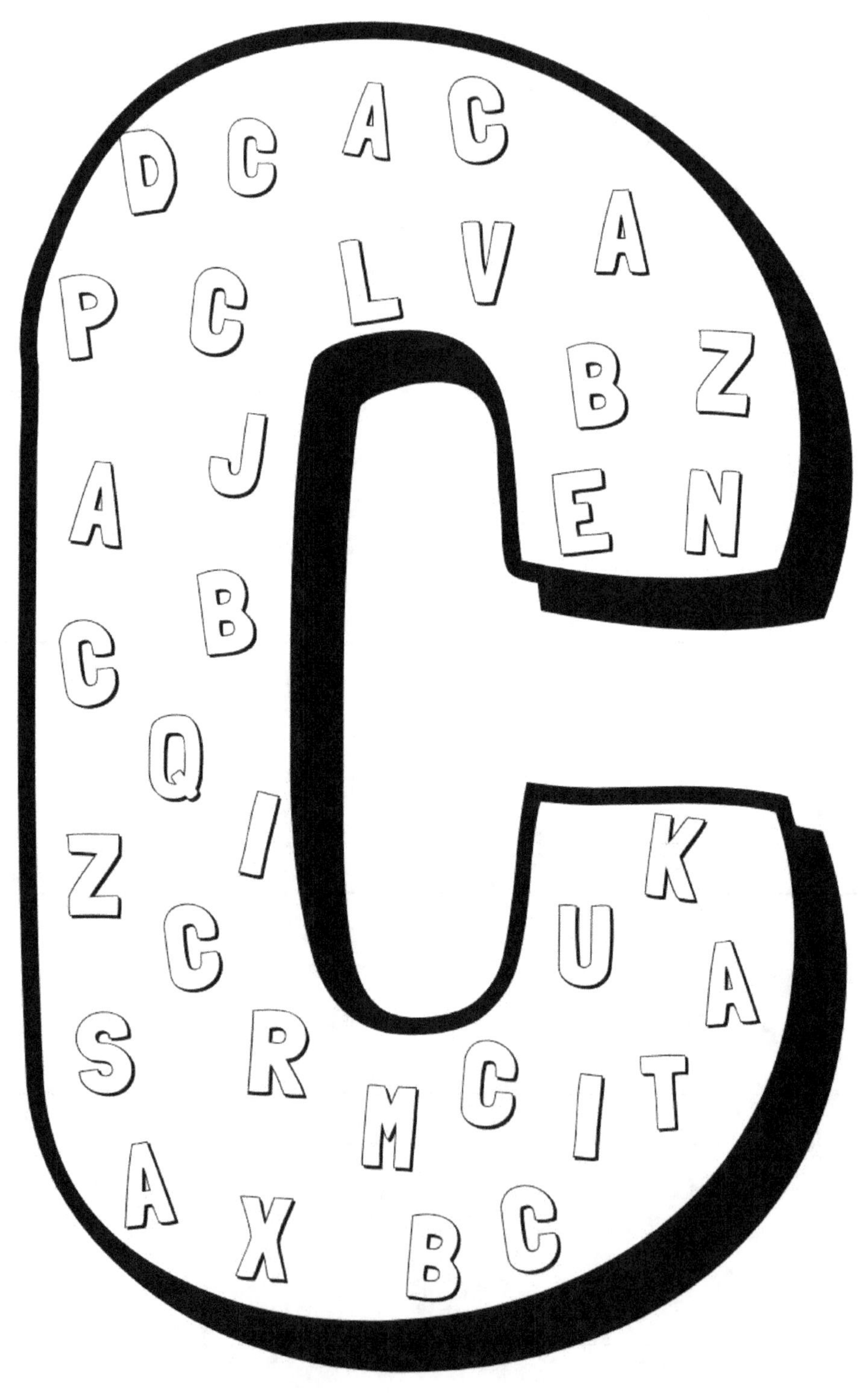

D d

D d

Letter Hunt

Find and color the letter D

E e
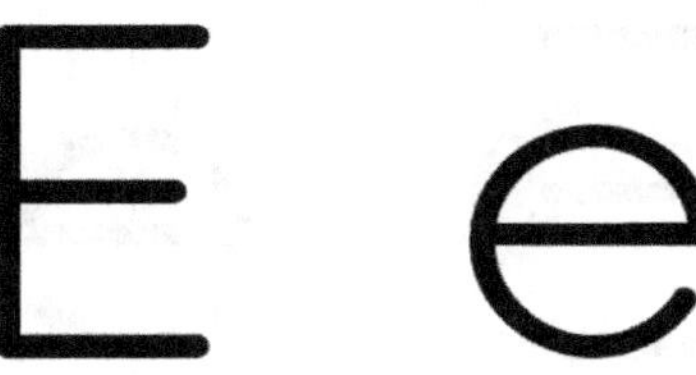

E e

Letter Hunt

Find and color the letter E

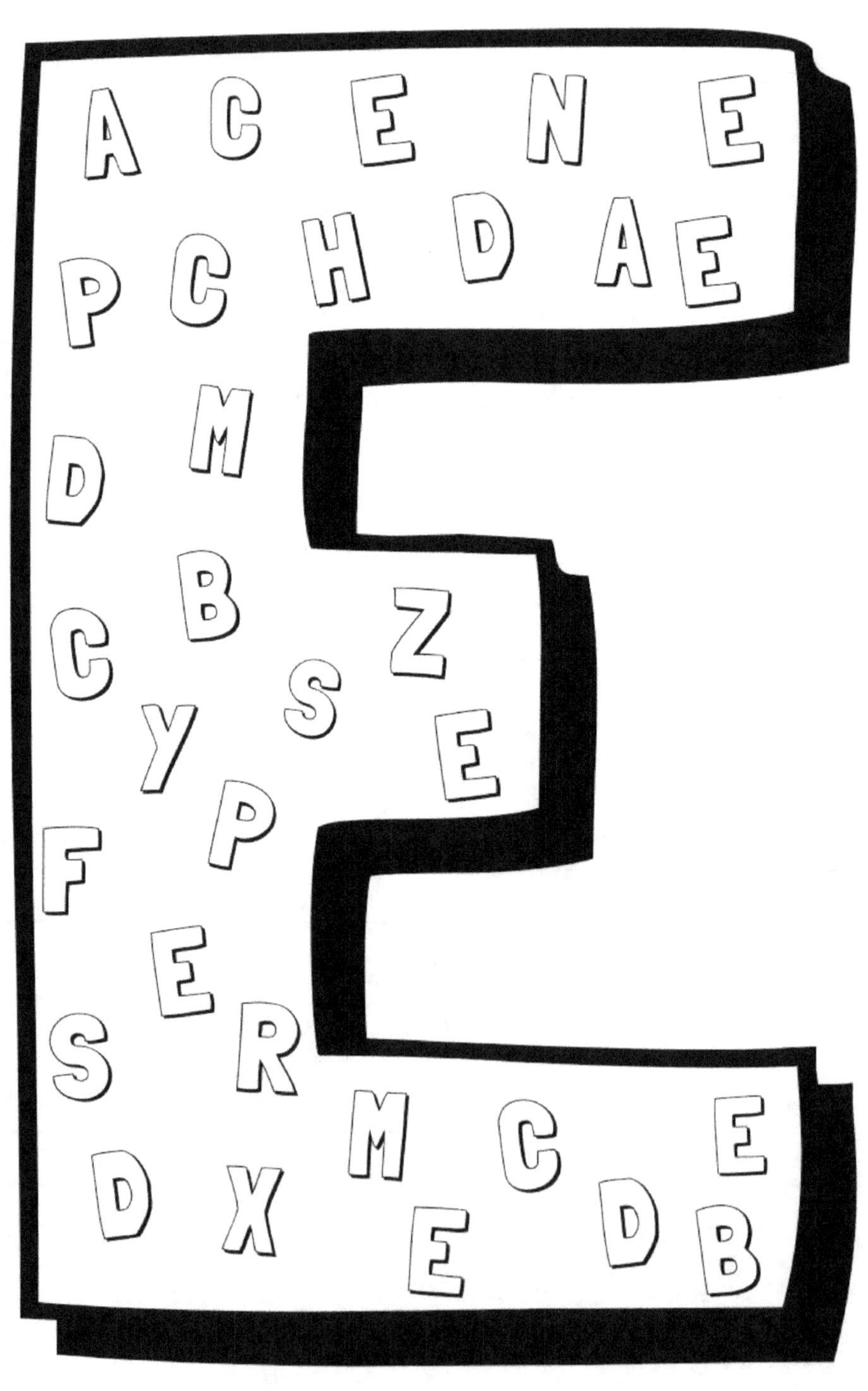

F f

Letter Hunt

Find and color the letter E

G g

G g

Letter Hunt

Find and color the letter G

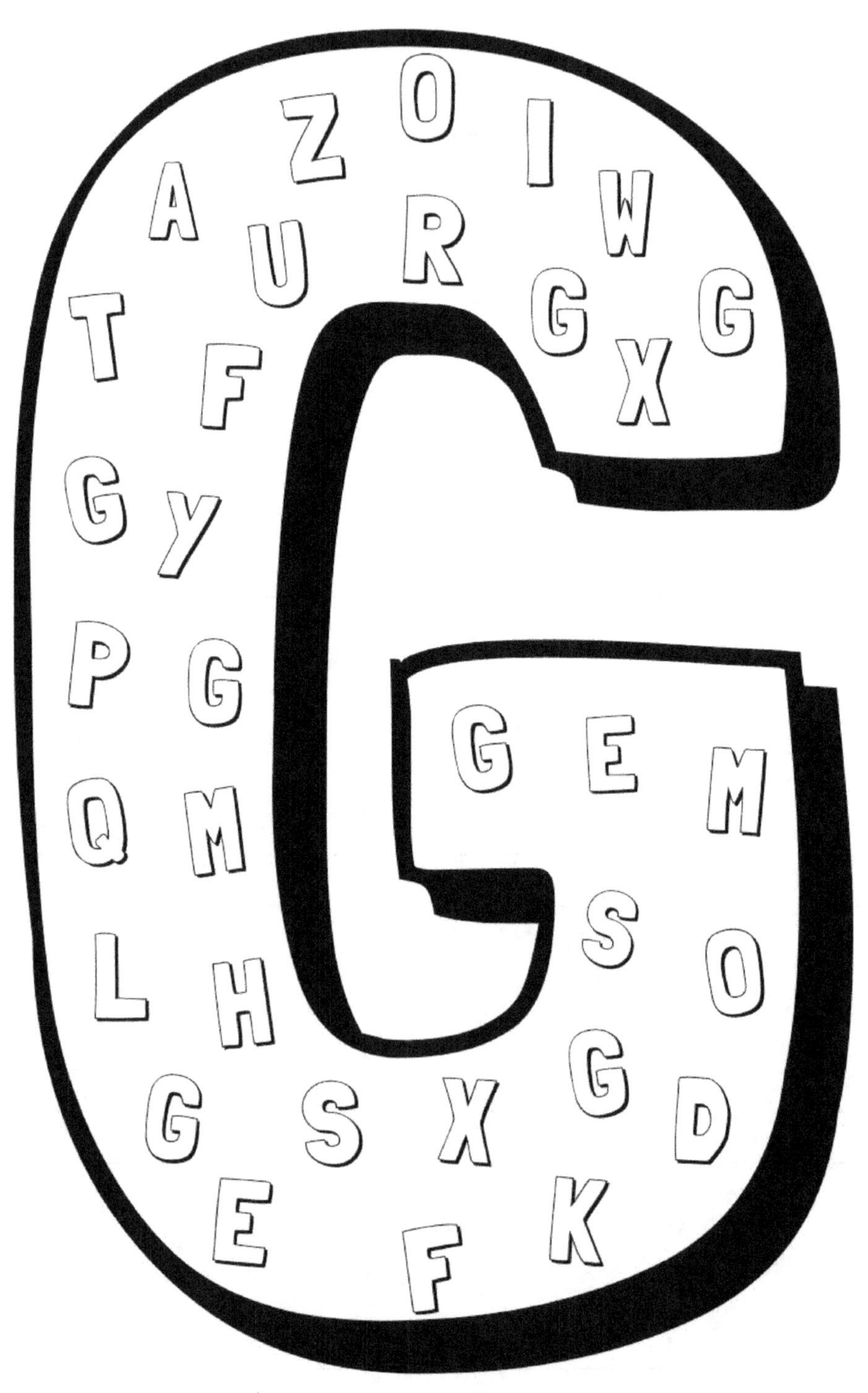

H h

Letter Hunt

Find and color the letter H

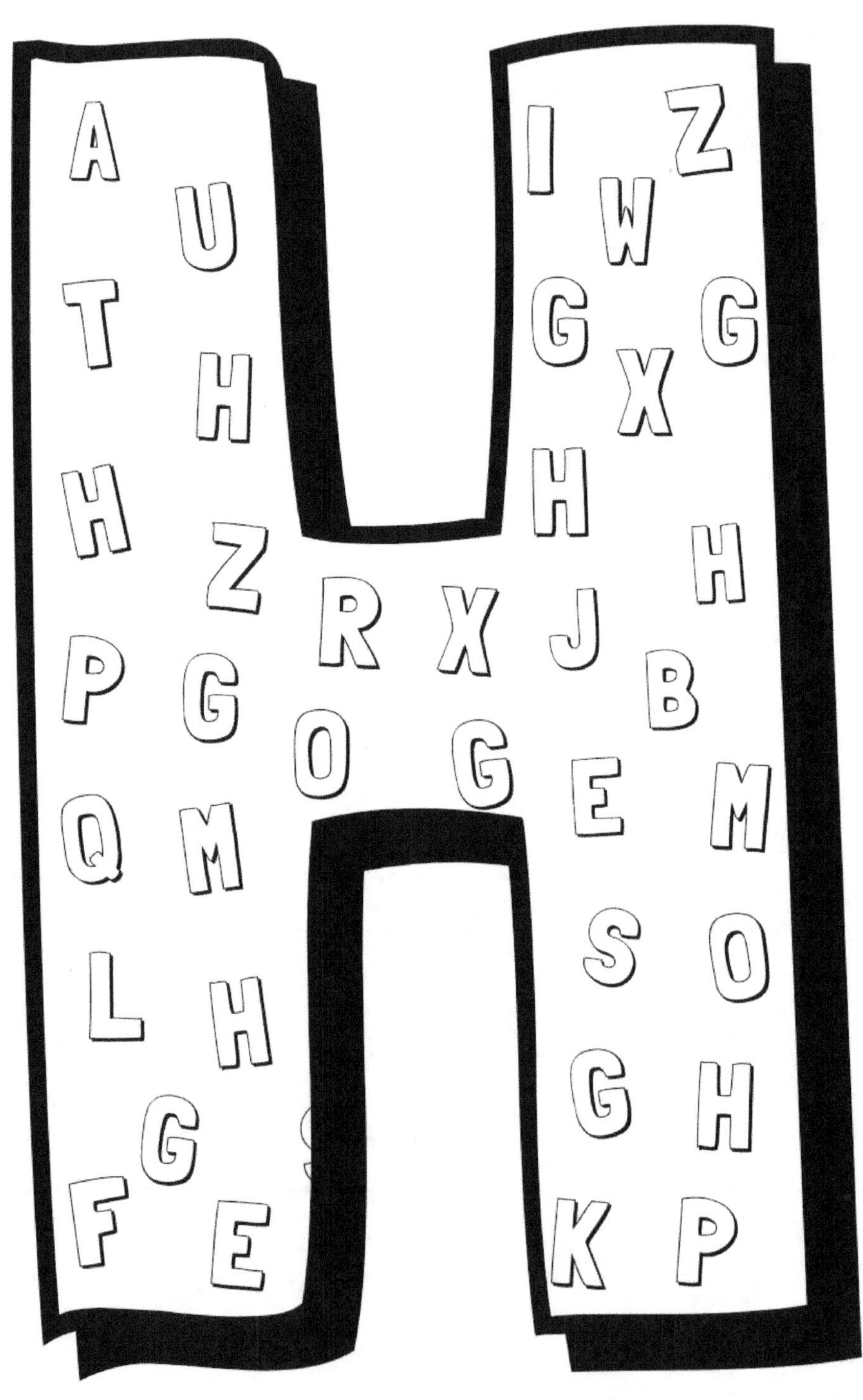

I i

I i

Letter Hunt

Find and color the letter I

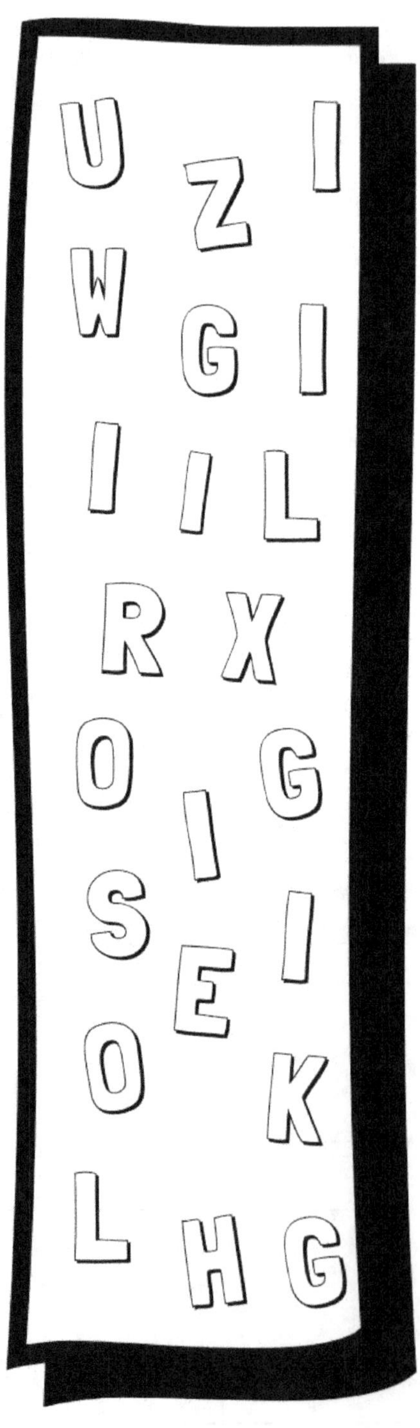

J j

Letter Hunt

Find and color the letter J

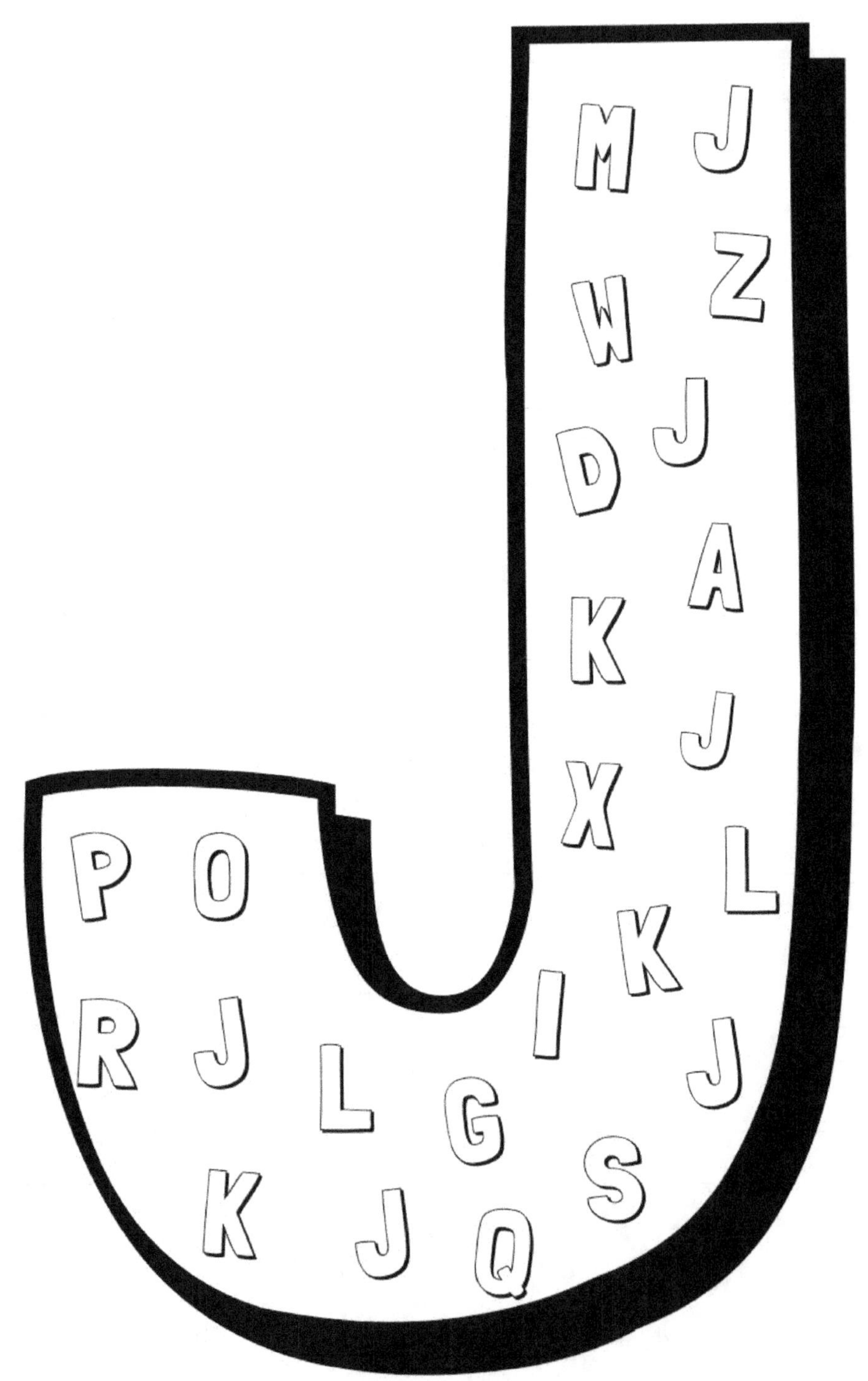

Letter Hunt

Find and color the letter K

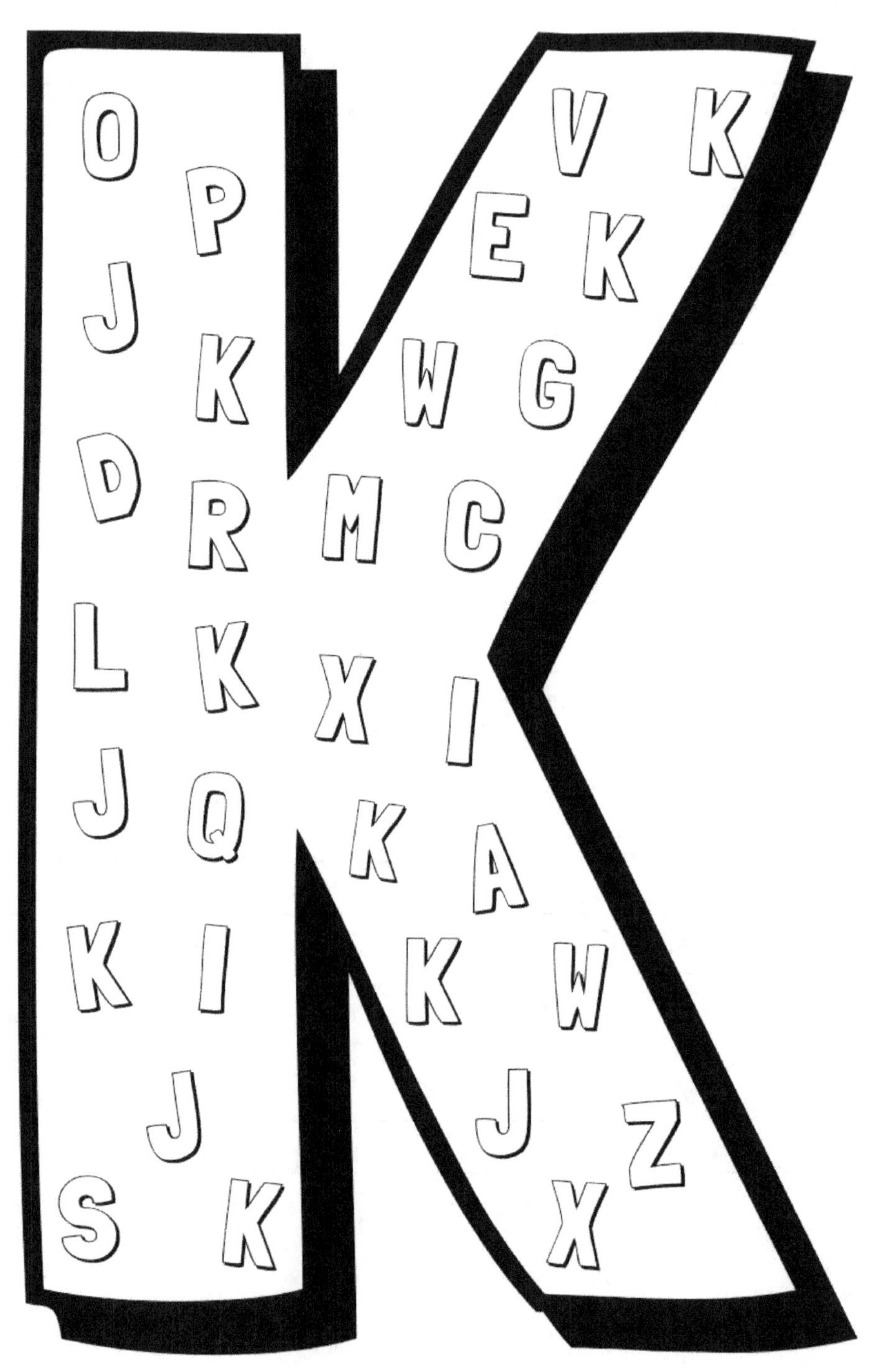

L l

L l

Letter Hunt

Find and color the letter L

M m

M m

Letter Hunt

Find and color the letter M

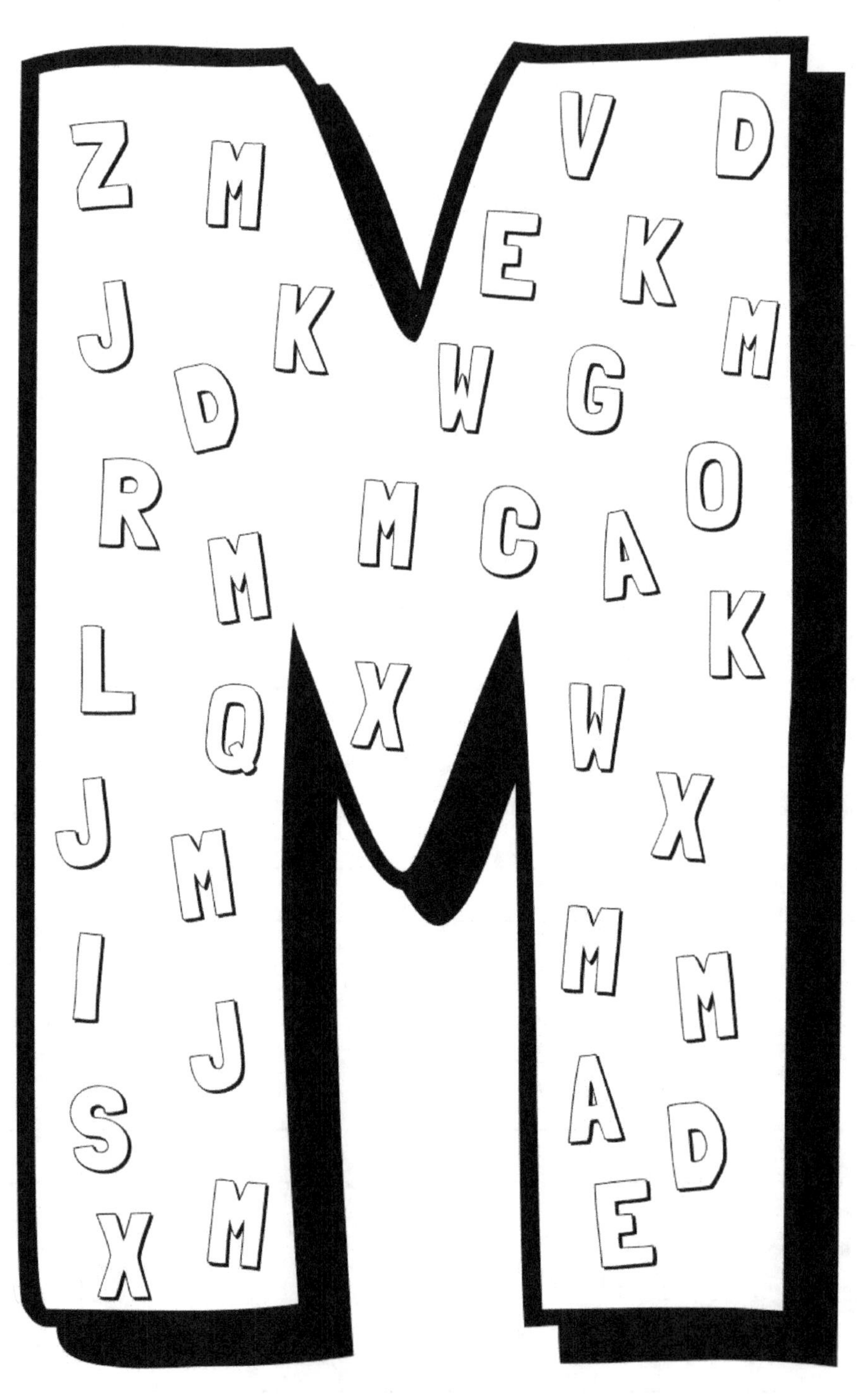

N n

N n

Letter Hunt

Find and color the letter N

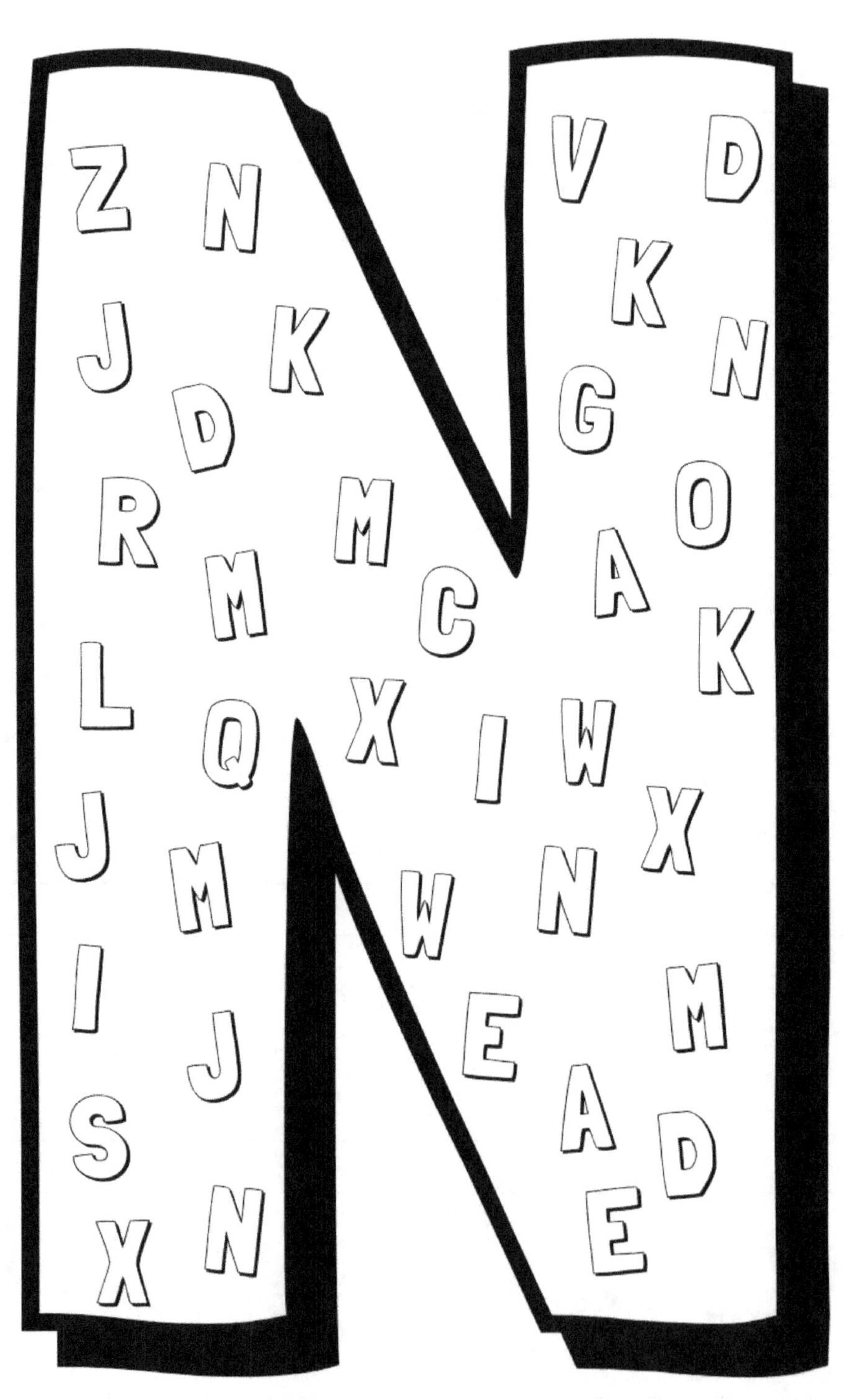

Letter Hunt

Find and color the letter O

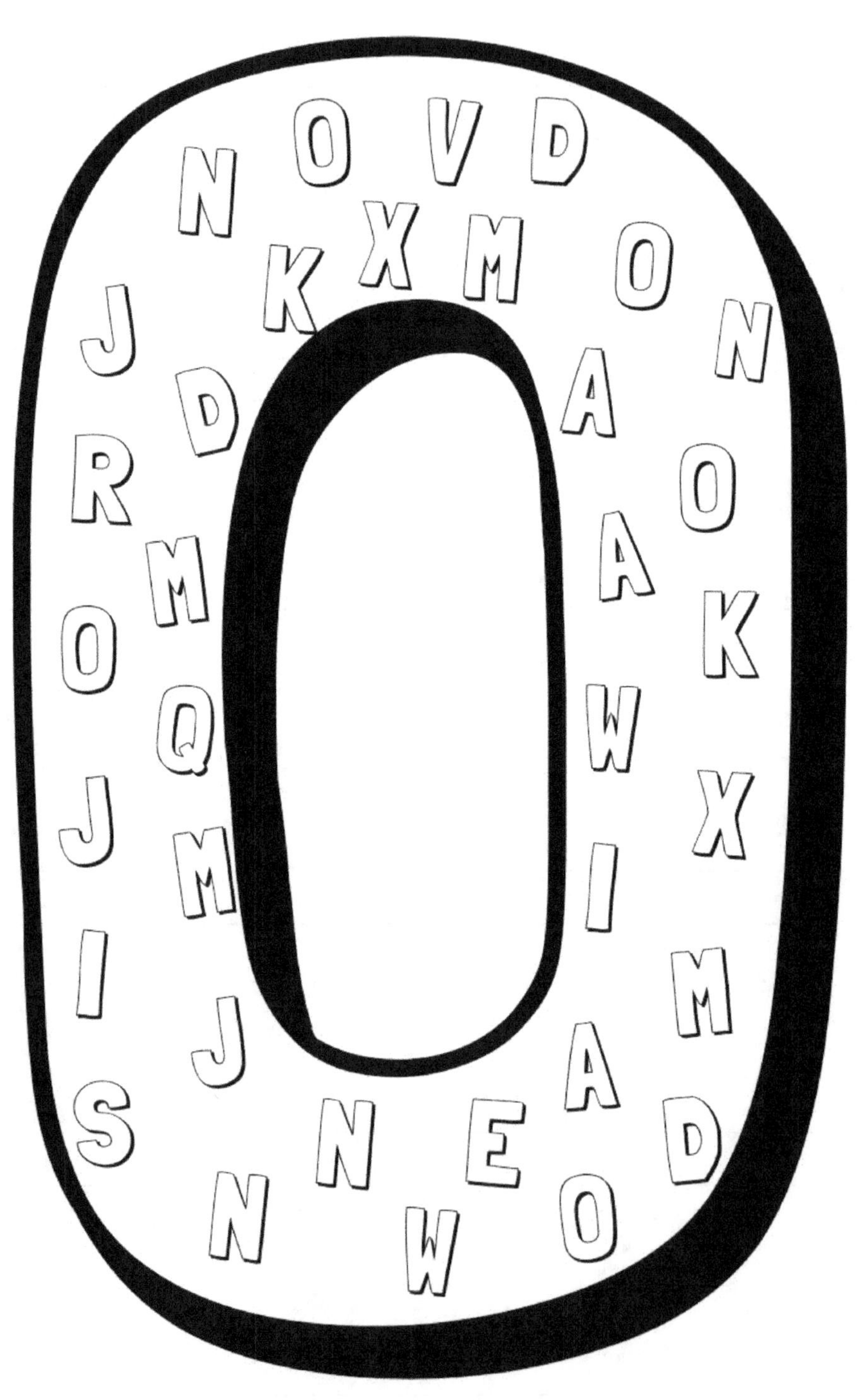

P p

P p

Letter Hunt

Find and color the letter P

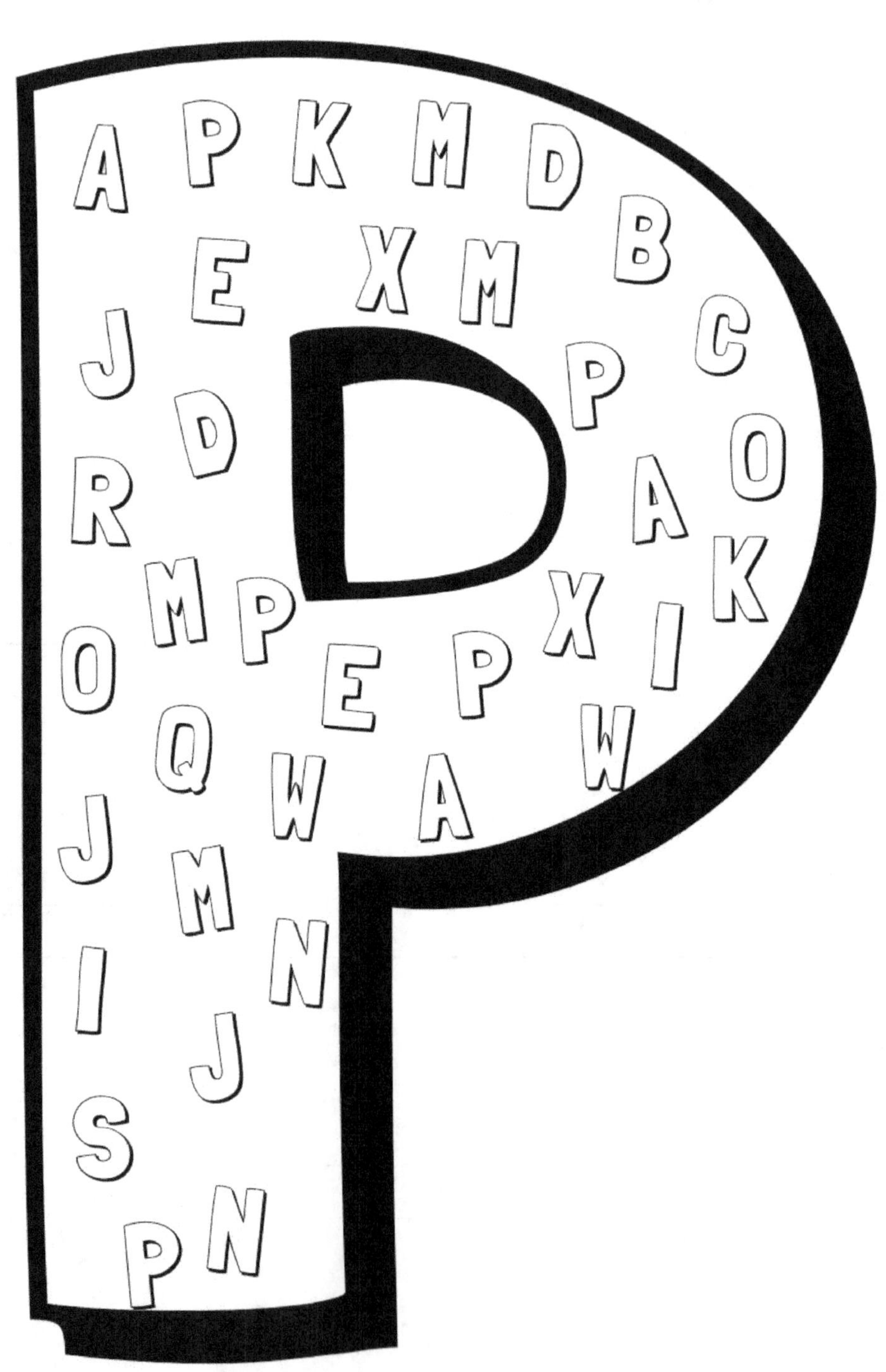

Q q

Q q

Letter Hunt

Find and color the letter Q

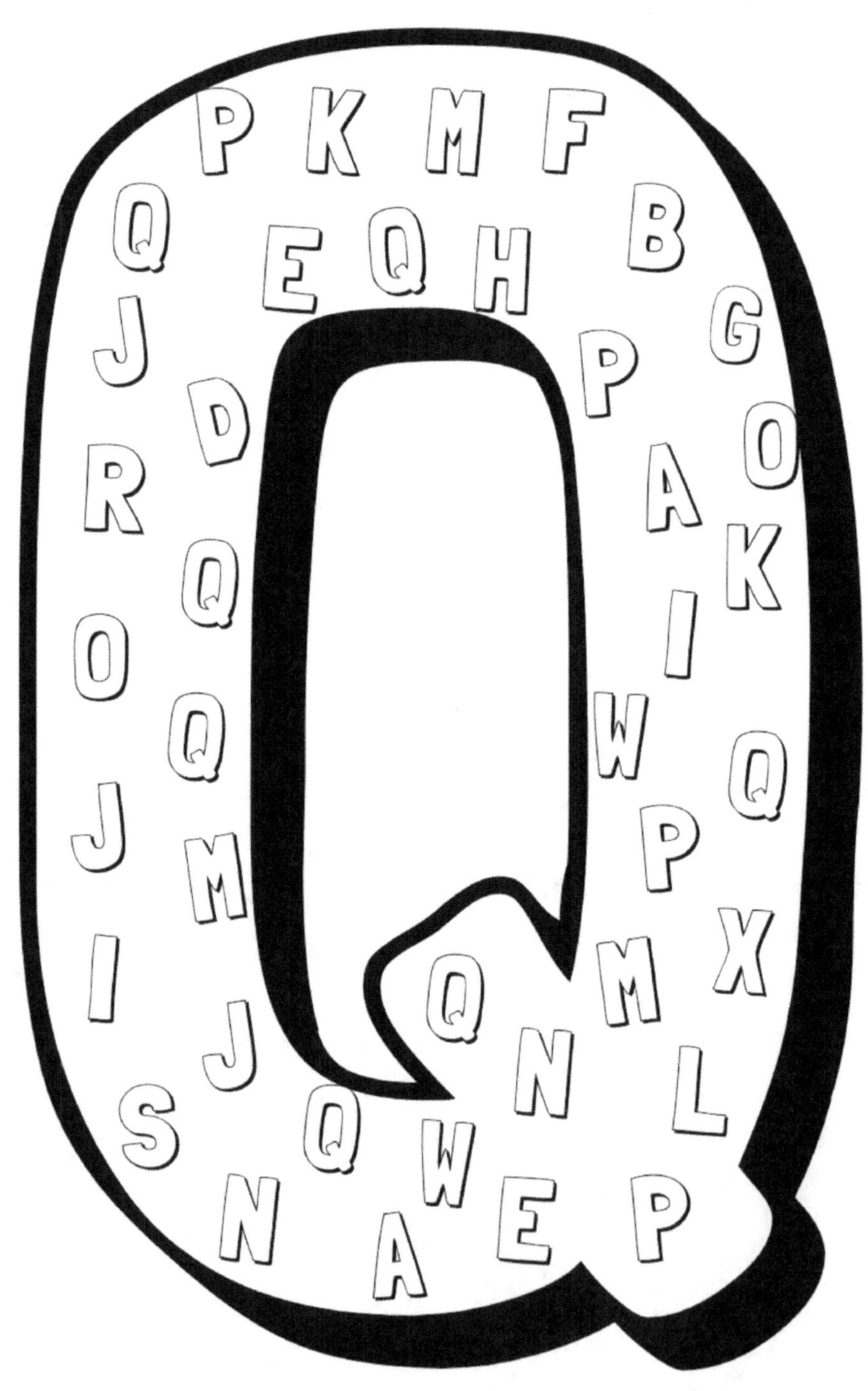

R r

R r

Letter Hunt

Find and color the letter R

S s

S s

Letter Hunt

Find and color the letter S

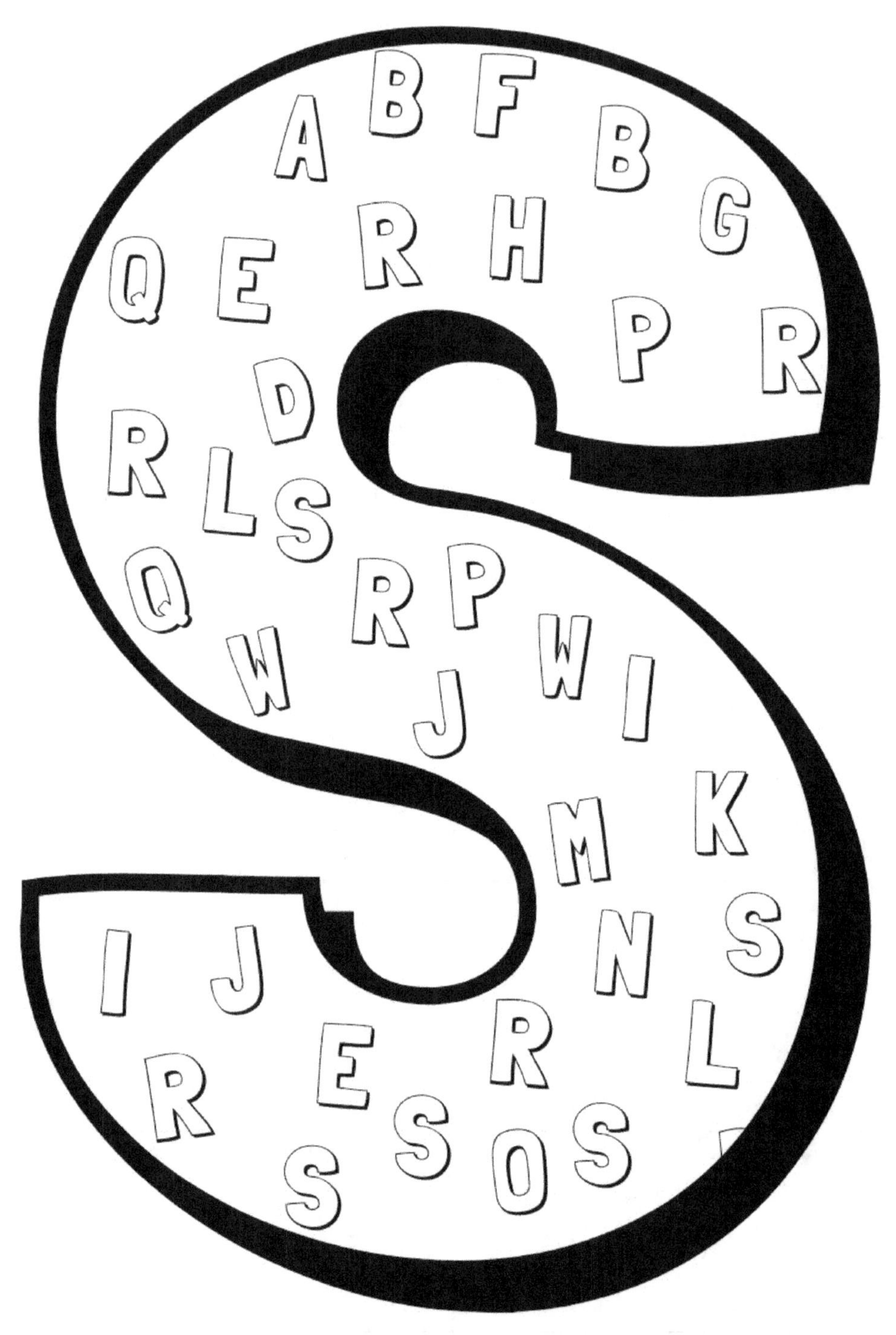

T t

T t

Letter Hunt

Find and color the letter T

U u

Letter Hunt

Find and color the letter U

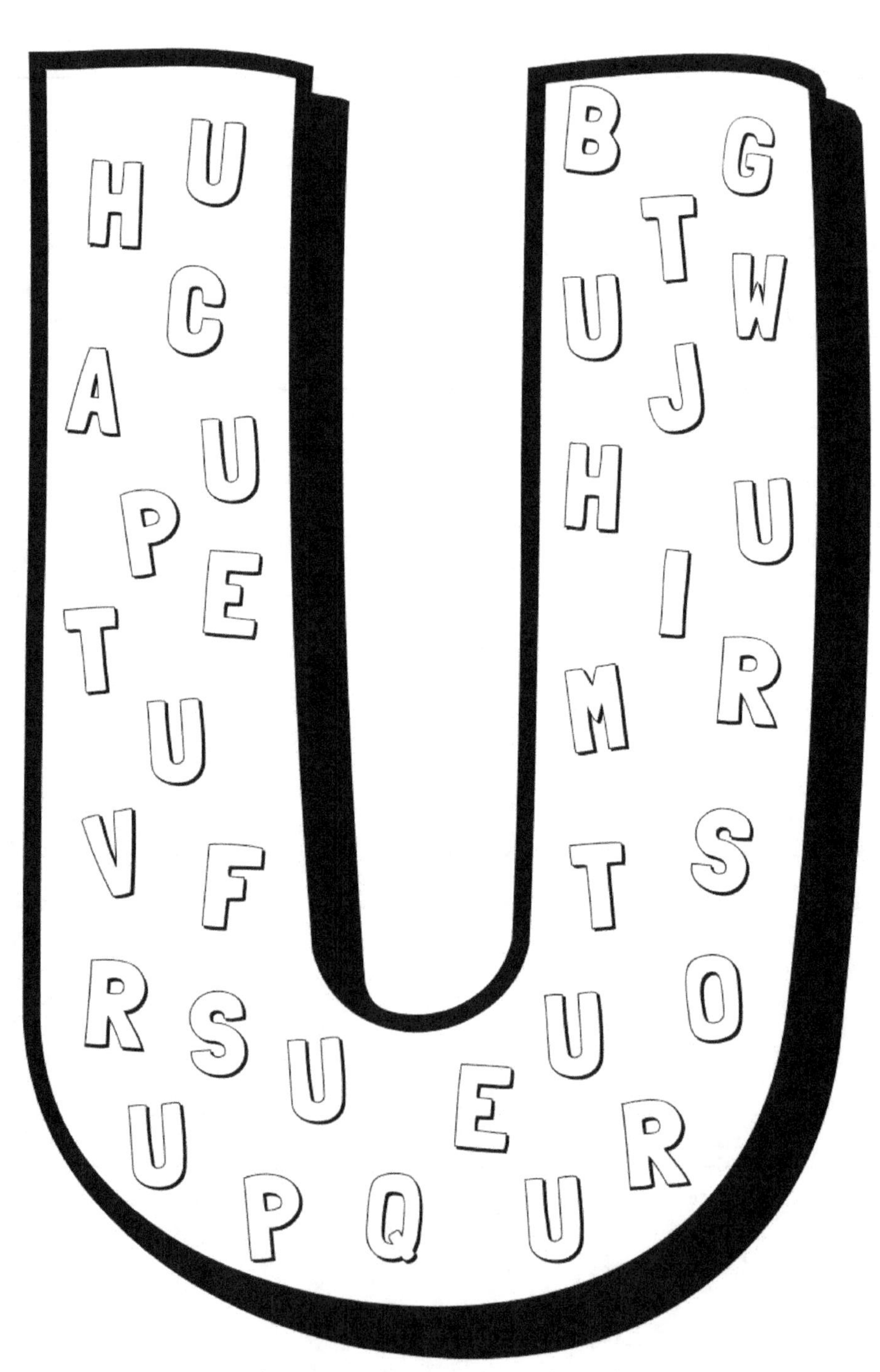

V v

Letter Hunt

Find and color the letter V

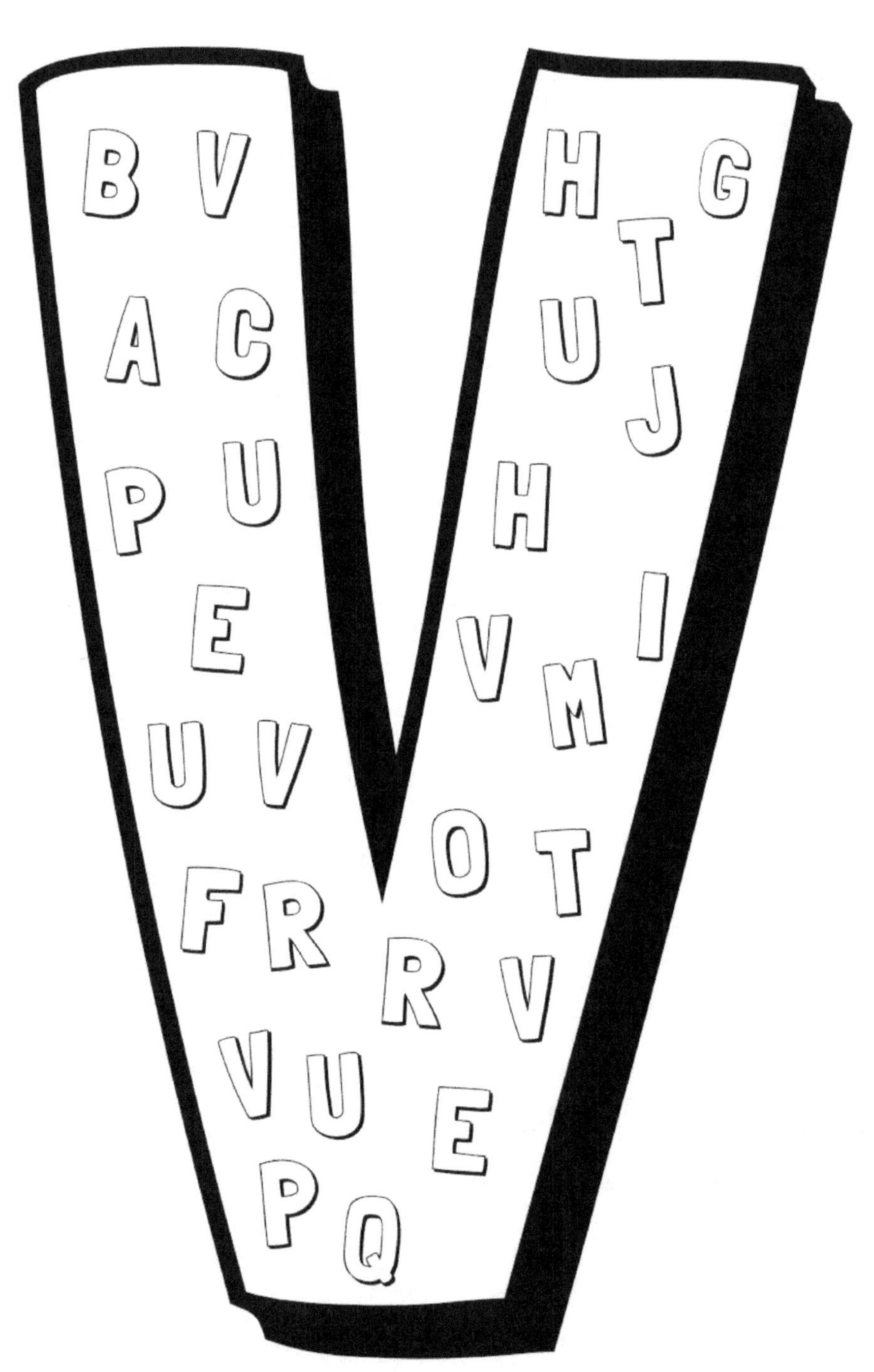

Ww

Letter Hunt

Find and color the letter W

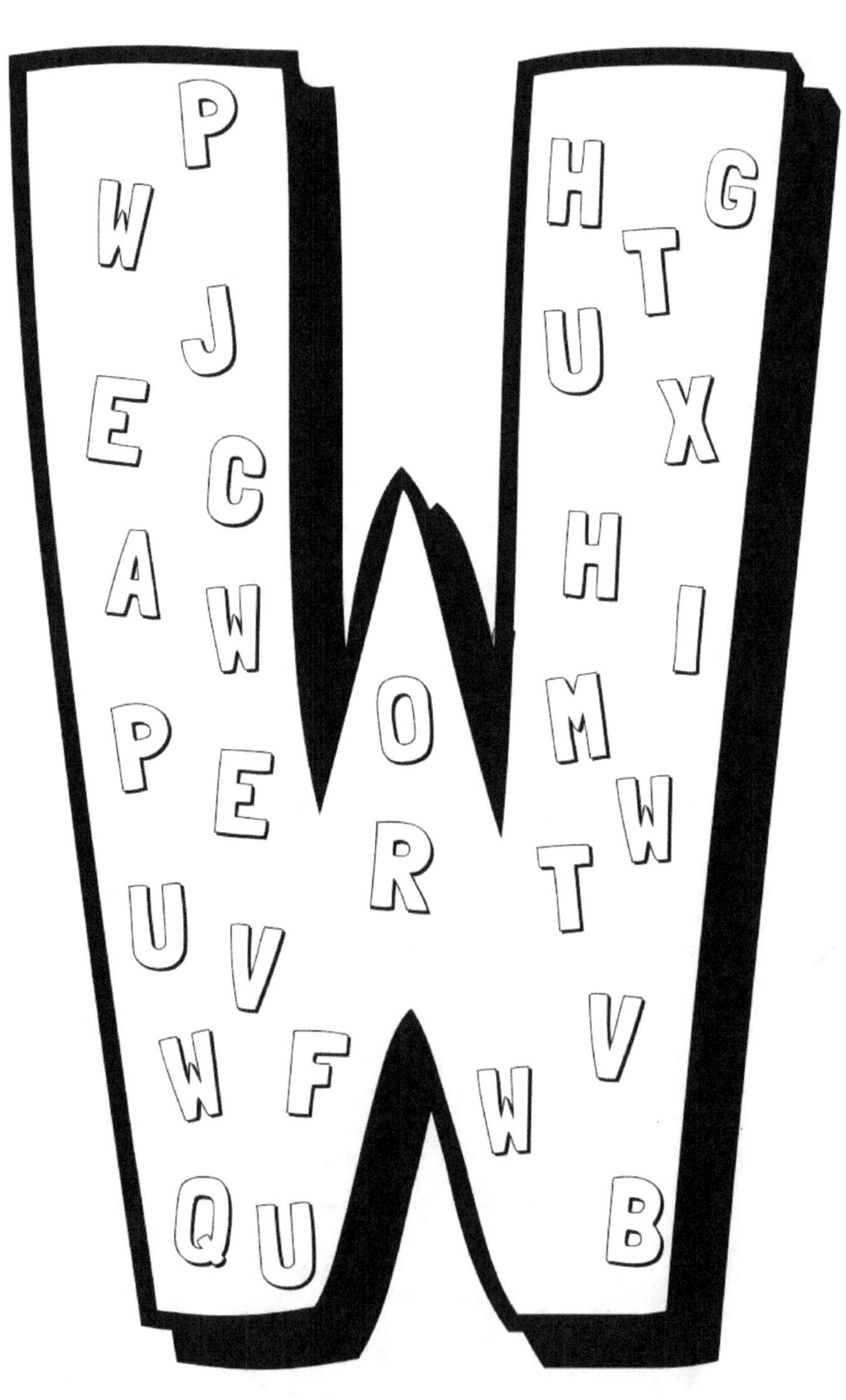

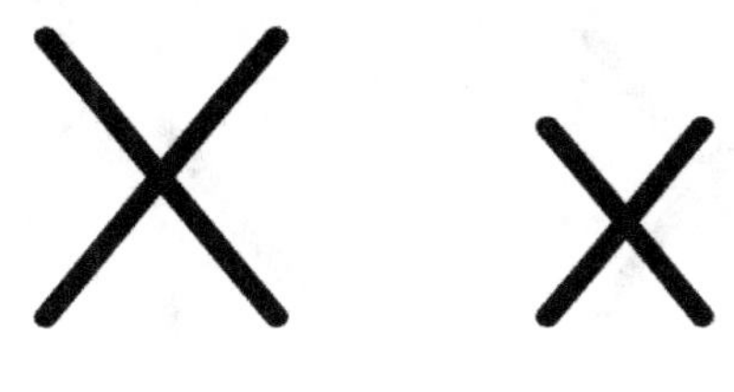

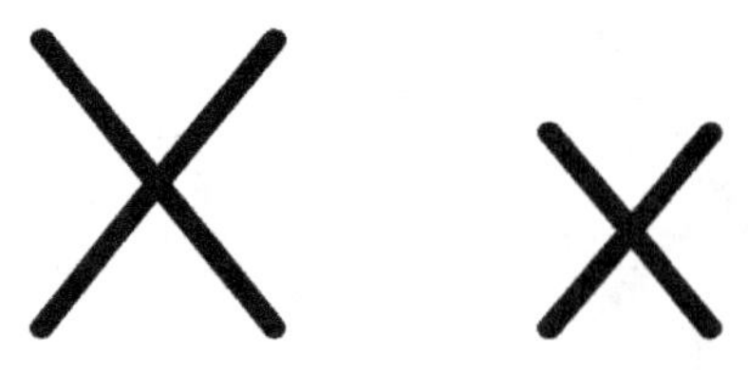

Letter Hunt

Find and color the letter X

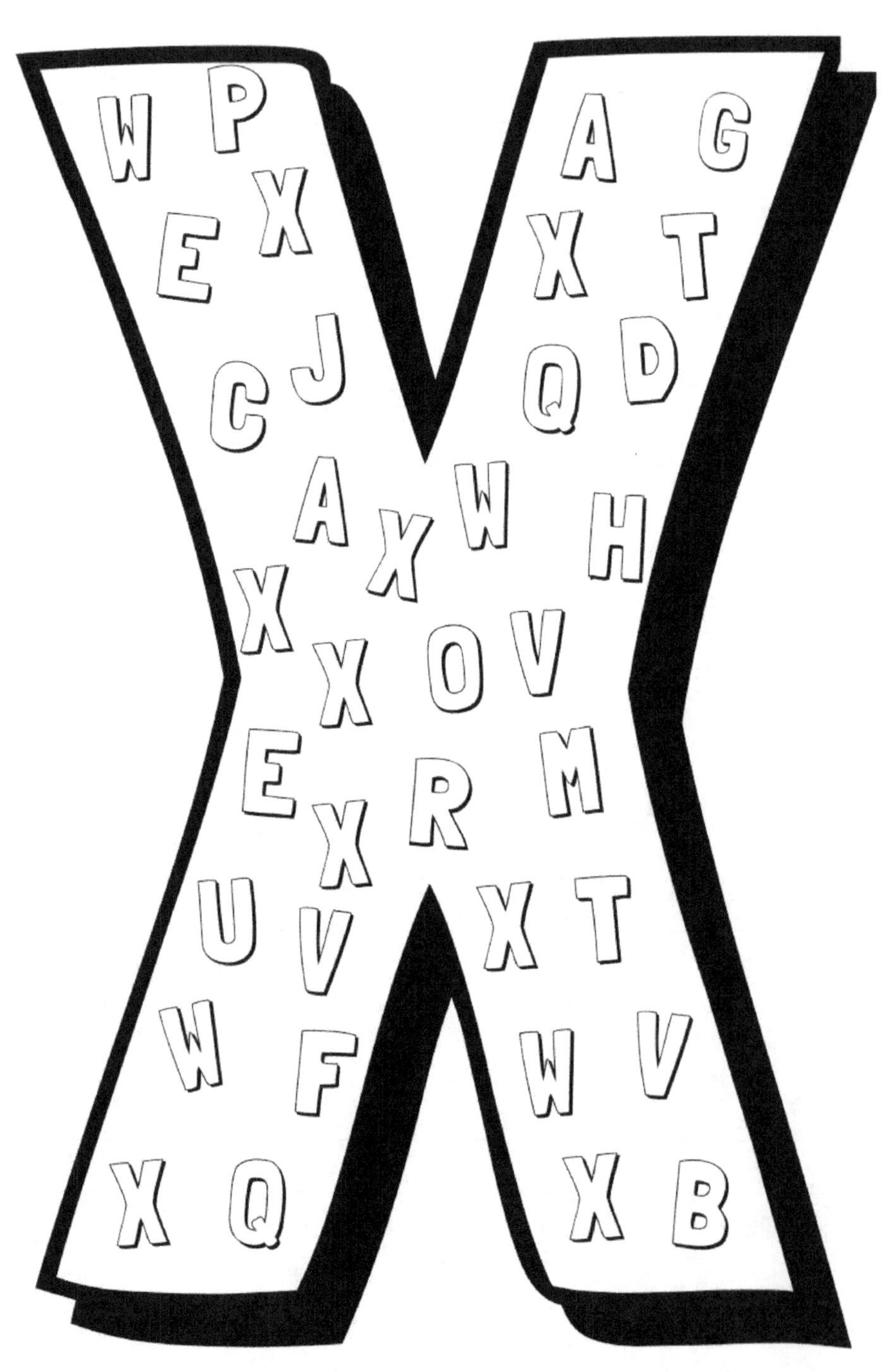

Y y

Y y

Letter Hunt

Find and color the letter Y

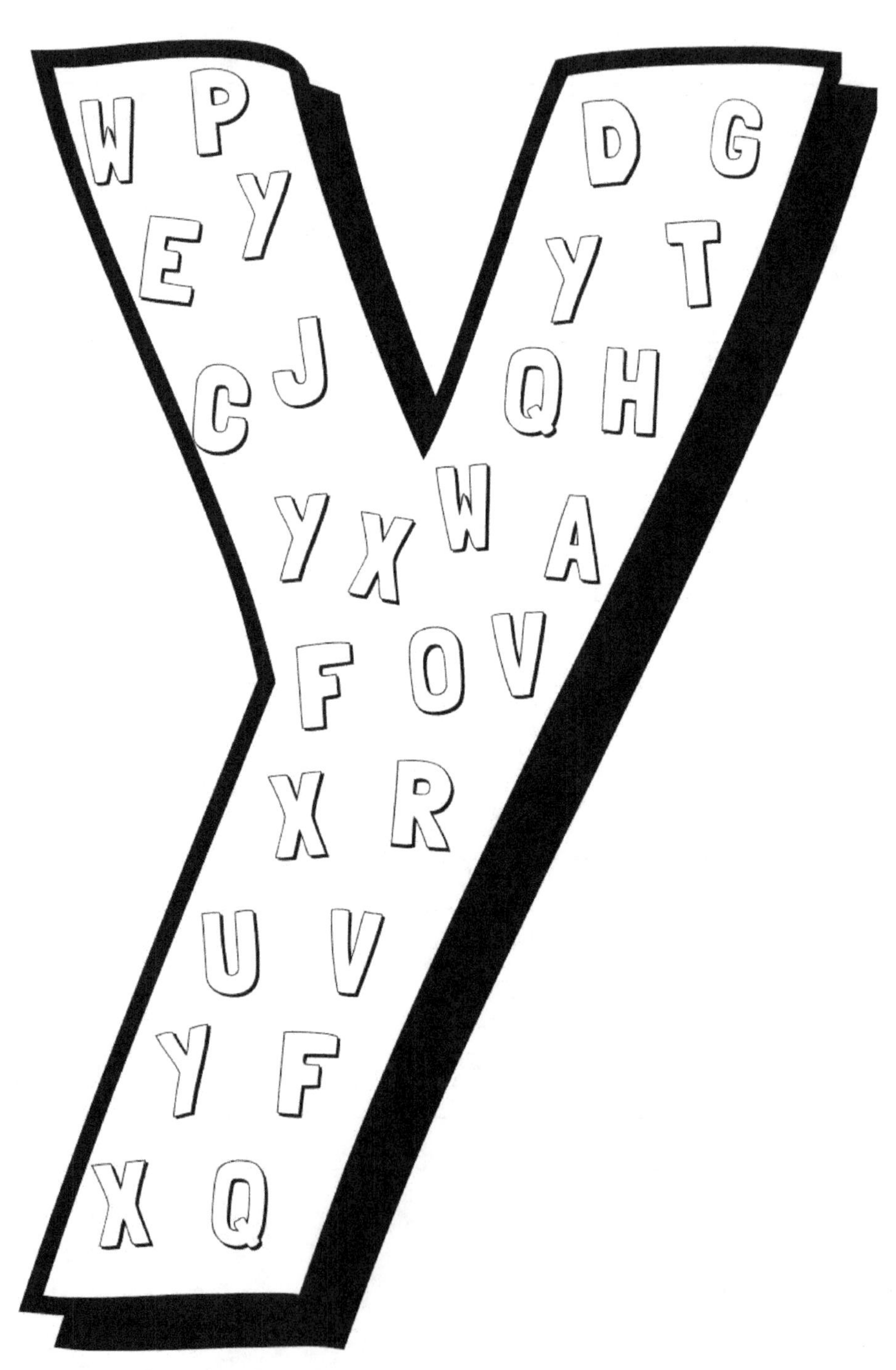

Z z

Z z

Letter Hunt

Find and color the letter Z

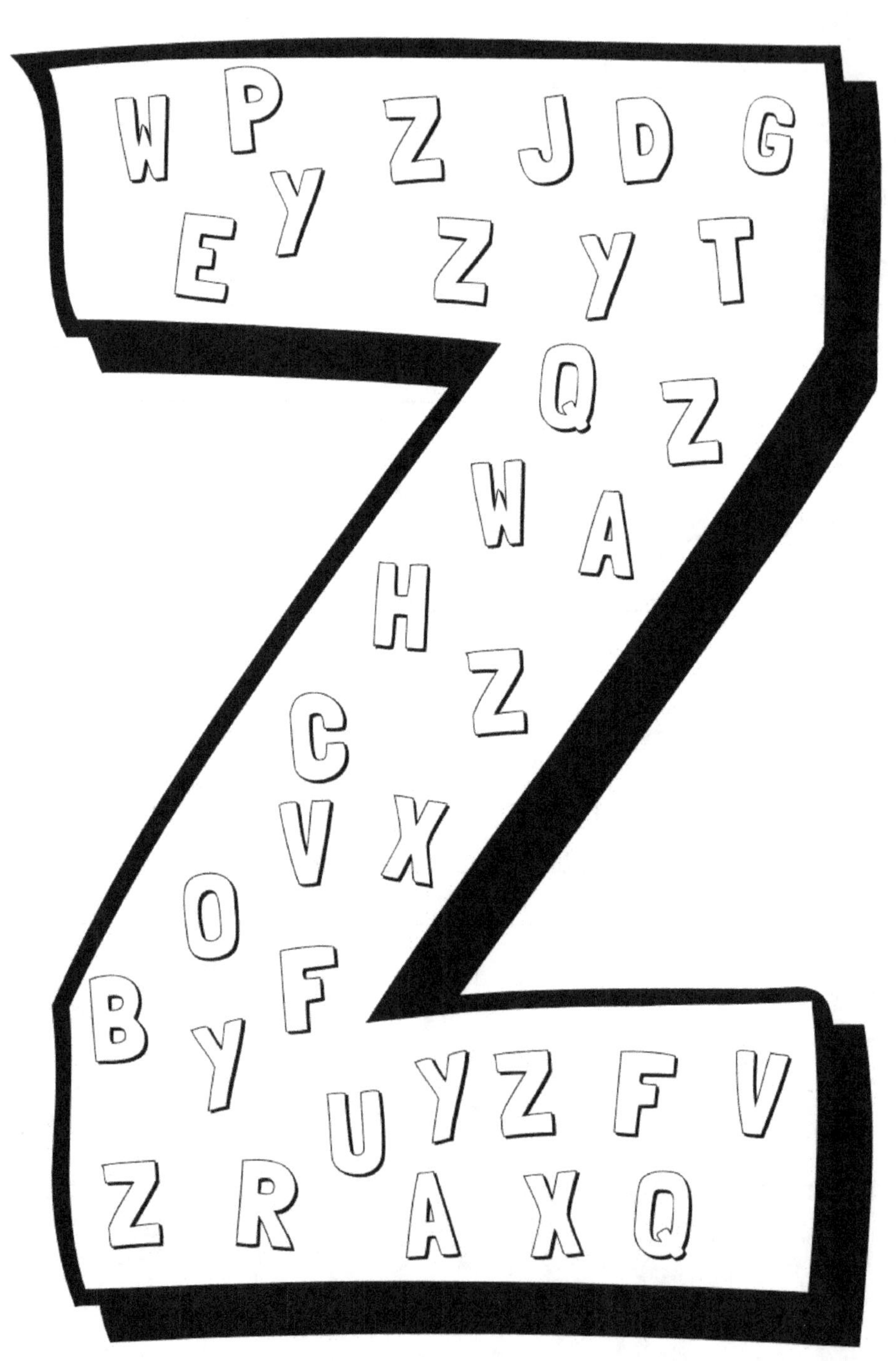

www.ingramcontent.com/pod-product-compliance
Lightning Source LLC
Chambersburg PA
CBHW081724250726
48657CB00010B/3117